CHURCH
Usher's Manual

A Systematic Approach to Church Ushering

CLYDE JACKSON

ISBN 979-8-89130-837-4 (paperback)
ISBN 979-8-89130-838-1 (digital)

Christian Faith Publishing
832 Park Avenue
Meadville, PA 16335
www.christianfaithpublishing.com

Printed in the United States of America

Designed for small, medium, large, and
megachurches/congregations

THIS BOOK BELONGS TO:

Name ____

Address ________________ State ________ Zip________

City ____

Telephone ____

Email ____

Contents

The Purpose

This book has prayerfully been written for the specific purpose of giving a clear insight into how to effectively serve as a church usher. Please be advised that nothing in this book takes the place of any instructions your pastor might have given you related to ushering in your church.

As you study this book, you will learn that at no time should a parishioner walk the aisle looking for seats. Assist them immediately. Ushers should be alert at all times.

This book, if necessary, can be used in conjunction with any other church ushering materials.

Church Usher's Personal Directory

Look in the Book!

God has given you a personal directory.
It is the BIBLE!
Do you look in it?

It should be in your home for education, in your hand for efficiency, in your head for enlightenment, and in your heart for enrichment. The Bible is so complete that nothing needs to be added to it. It is a timely help in times of need.

For comfort in times of sorrow, read Romans 8:26–28.

For relief in times of suffering, read 2 Corinthians 12:8–10.

For protection in times of danger, read Psalm 91.

For peace in times of turmoil, read Philippians 4:6–7.

For guidance in times of decisions, read Proverbs 3:5–6.

For strength in times of temptation, read 1 Corinthians 10:13.

For courage, read 1 John 1:7–9.

For help in times of death, read Psalm 23.

Whatever your problem, look in the Book.

Guidelines and Illustrations

The following should be stressed by presidents or instructors:

- No chewing gum
- Hair groomed
- Clean shaven
- Suit pressed
- Shoes shined
- Clean shirt and tie
- Proper uniform

Church ushers should consider the following:

- Be on time
- Never leave a post without permission
- Do not assume authority
- Concentrate on the services
- Pay special attention to Guests
- Adequate supply of envelopes, hymn books, bulletins, and Bibles
- Know the order of service
- Know duties and responsibilities
- Follow instructions

Church ushers should also consider the following:

- Be proud to be a church usher
- Have a pleasant attitude toward the church

- Engage pleasant conversation
- Maintain pleasant facial expressions
- Stay prayerful

When sitting on the right, extend the right arm, palm open, fingers together. When sitting on the left, extend the left arm open, fingers together.

Head Usher

The usher who is to direct the ushers for a particular service may be referred to as the head usher, usher leader, or director of ushers. The usher who directs the ushers while they are serving in the aisles should be referred to as the lead usher.

All church edifices you enter, please refer to your aisles as A, B, C, D, etc. starting from right to left. Starting from your right, place ushers in the aisle accordingly when necessary.

After ushers have been given their assigned aisles, the head usher will spread both hands slightly, indicating, "Take your assigned position."

Aisle ushers will space themselves in the aisle, turn, and face the rear of the sanctuary.

Bringing ushers from the aisle, the head usher will raise both hands, face high, palms inward.

Head usher to aisle usher requesting available seats: both hands face high with the first finger of each hand pointing upward.

Head usher to doorkeepers indicating no one is to enter: both hands chest high clasped together.

Please inform all ushers that signs are to be given, smoothly and quickly, not readily noticed by the congregation.

Following are qualities common to successful church usher instructors:

- Thorough knowledge of the subject
- Ability to put subject across
- Interest in training
- Patience and trust
- Fair and impartial
- Understanding of people and their learning ability

- Ability to lead rather than drive
- Pleasing disposition
- Prepare a lesson plan for each training session
- Command respect and confidence
- Employ simple and correct language
- Ability to give friendly encouragement to slow learners

Ushers and Head Usher Working Together

Before a sign is given, the aisle usher and doorkeeper will make eye contact with the head usher. Therefore, all ushers must remain alert at all times. Head usher will also follow the same procedure (eye contact). All signs should be given as quickly as possible.

Ushers serving in the aisle for seating purposes and at the door will stand in a relaxed position with right hand over left at the waist (male and female).

Aisle ushers during scripture and prayer: altogether will turn and face the rostrum, remain in a relaxed position, slightly bow their heads, and when over, return as they were.

Church ushers operate more effectively when using silent, distant communication with the use of signs.

Readiness: no learning takes place until the trainer's mind is receptive to the impulse received.

DIAGRAM

Offering or Communion

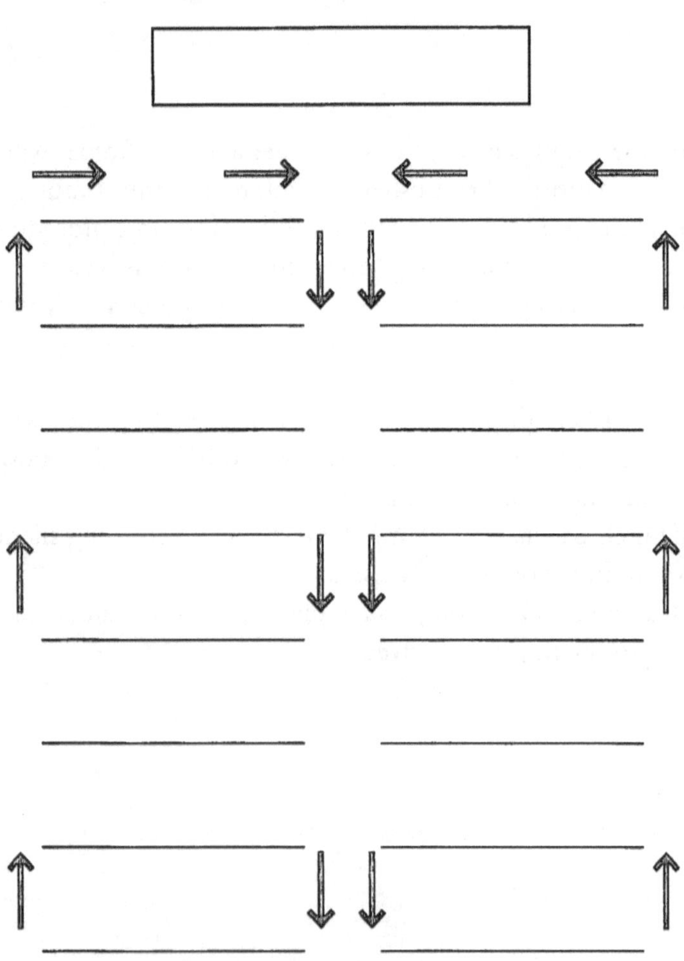

Directing for Offering, Communion, Etc.

When passing trays for offering, ushers will stay together as they move up and down the aisle.

When marching for offering or communion, use two ushers, one to lead parishioners and escort them back to their seats and one to escort them from their seats.

Please always direct the audience in a manner where they will return to their same seats.

How beautiful are those who serve as
doorkeepers in the House of God.

Hints and Suggestions for Ushers, Instructors, and Presidents to Use before Cross-Training Session of Meeting

Encourage ushers to attend Sunday-school class and Bible-study class. The Bible is a book for all seasons. It is referred to as the good book, the holy book. The more you read it, the sweeter it gets.

The Bible, without a doubt, is truly inspired by God.

If troubled or discouraged, read Psalm 3, Isaiah 26:3, Deuteronomy 33:27.

If in sickness, read Psalm 103, Isaiah 53.

If lonesome and restless, read Psalms 23 and 27.

If bitter or critical, read 1 Corinthians 1:3.

When worried, read Matthew 6:19, 34.

When feeling blue, read Psalm 34.

When God seems far away, read Psalm 139.

When leaving home for work or travel, read Psalm 121, 107:23–31.

Please enforce the use of common sense:

Ushers are to be alert at all times. The head usher is watching all ushers, and all ushers should be watching the head usher. Carry these through with you:

Live for today. Dream for tomorrow. Learn from yesterday.

Don't find fault; find a remedy.

Helpful Hints for Usher Board Presidents

1. Don't fail to begin meeting on time.
2. Don't say, "You heard the motion." State the motion.
3. Don't say, "It has been moved." Say, "It is moved and seconded."
4. Don't repeat the motion offered by a member and then ask if there is a second. Motions requiring a second should be seconded before being stated by the presiding officer.
5. Don't omit to take the negative vote on every motion.
6. Don't omit to declare the result of every vote.
7. Don't ever entertain a motion that one person cast the ballot.
8. Don't allow the meeting to drag but make every effort to expedite the transaction of business.
9. Don't talk too much.
10. Don't fail to have all records kept in books belonging to the organization.
11. Do call the meeting to order promptly.
12. Do preserve order at all times.
13. Do entertain one piece of business at a time.
14. Do ensure full and free discussion.
15. Do keep your temper.
16. Do use general consent whenever possible
17. Do quit running things when your term of office is over.

Usher board president, it's very important that you communicate closely with your pastor. Meet with him/her to find out what orders or information they might have for the ushers also on special days and what orders they might have for visiting ministries.

Putting a Motion through the House

There are eight steps necessary to complete a motion.

1. Rise and address the chair, "Madam President." Wait for recognition.
2. Receive recognition—chair calls you by name or nods in your direction.
3. Make your motion. "I move to," or "I move that."
4. Another member seconds the motion, showing that more than one member of the assembly wishes the matter considered. You need not rise to say, "I second it."
5. The chair states the motion (repeats the motion).
6. The chair asks for discussion if the motion is debatable.
7. The chair puts a motion to vote. "All in favor, say, 'Aye.' Those opposed, say, 'No,'"
8. The chair announces the result.

If the chair is in doubt of the result, she or he should say, "The chair is in doubt," then call for a rising vote. A motion goes into effect immediately when the chair states the result, unless a time element was included in the motion. A motion remains in effect until executed or rescinded.

Purpose or Objectives of Parliamentary Rule

1. Conduct an orderly meeting.
2. Maintain justice.
3. Expedite business.

Principles of Parliamentary Rule

1. Courtesy and justice of all
2. Consideration of one thing at a time
3. Right of the majority to rule
4. Right of the minority to be heard
5. Right of the absentee to be protected

From Author to All Church Ushers

This service that you perform is not only supplying the needs of God's people, but is also overflowing in many expressions of thanks to God.

—2 Corinthians 9:12

And certainly, we thank God for your gift of service. As parishioners, we don't always respond to your warm greetings with a thank-you, but it doesn't seem to matter, for you always say, "You're welcome," by the joy you exude each Sunday as we enter our various edifices.

When we're handed a church paper or shown to our seats, we don't always say, "Thank you," but you continue to say, "You're welcome," for each Sunday, you can be counted on to perform these tasks with unequaled enthusiasm.

When you're asked to be a delivery person of messages or find an escort to take a tiny tot to the washroom, we don't always say, "Thank you," but you always say, "You're welcome," for you go about your duties with the warmth that permits us to continue to impose on you.

Your service to us is always appreciated, for our needs are truly being met. We do say thanks to God for you, and he, too, says, "You're welcome," for he continues to give you the health, strength, energy, and love for his people to continue to serve.

We say, "God bless you, and may you continue to brighten our lives in your special ways."

Church Nurse's Guidelines and Responsibilities

1. Serving in church worship services, funerals, programs, state and national conventions, and whenever and wherever needed in your community.
2. Set up a workshop with the Red Cross for CPR and basic first aid. To be a church nurse, you do not have to be an LPN or RN.
3. In your church, try to get to know your members with diabetes and heart conditions. No medication is to be given by us at any time. You can assist them by giving water to take their own medication. You may take blood pressure, temperature, and pulse.
4. For funerals, you are only there for moral support or emergency. Do not take the family seats, and do not fan. Allow them to hold your hands; reassure them that you are there if needed.
5. If a person is in the spirit, just stand by for support.
6. Be kind and courteous. Report for duty on time to assemble for prayer.

Sign: Request for Church Nurse. Place the right hand on top of the head.

Tribute for a Deceased Usher

And I heard a voice from heaven saying unto me, write, blessed are the dead which die in the Lord from henceforth: Yea, saith the spirit, that they may rest from their labors; and their works do follow them.

—Revelation 14:13

Sister _____________ or Brother _____________ was a dedicated church usher. She or he possessed those Christian ideals and respect of all church ushers who knew her or him. She or he has left living examples of loving service worthy of our emulation.

_____________ is not dead but has passed beyond the mist that blinds us here into the new larger life. Our lives are unfinished books, of which we are writing day by day. When completed, others will read it and remember what we did and had to say.

May this tribute bring some comfort to the relatives and friends of _____________.

Respectfully submitted by _____________.

* All ushers will stand while the tribute is being read.

Increasing Your Church Membership through Church Ushers

It is very important that, as church ushers and greeters, we learn names and greet each parishioner, usher, and guest by name. You will be surprised how it will improve relations between ushers, parishioners, and guests. Have a church fellowship other than Sunday worship services, using name tags to learn members' names (if necessary).

**Head Usher instructing aisle usher
to turn and face the rostrum**

Right hand face high, palm outward.

Relaxed Position

**Head Usher to aisle usher
reuqesting available seats**

*Both hands face high with first finger
of each hand pointing upward*

**Head Usher to doorkeepers indicating
no one is to enter**

Both hands chest high clasped together

Seating On Left

When seating on left – extend left arm
palm open, fingers closed.

Bringing Ushers from Aisle

*The head usher will raise both hands
face high palms inward.*

**Aisle Usher request for
contribution envelope**

*Left and right hand at waist,
as if putting money in envelope.*

Seating on Right

*When seating on right – extend right arm
palm open, fingers together.*

Aisle Usher requesting someone come for message

*Left hand up to forehead using
index finger touching it.*

Aisle Usher request for church bulletins

*Raise both hands waist high, palms open, hands together,
bow head slightly indicating reading.*

Aisle Usher indicating available seats

Both hands waist high, palm open.

Aisle Usher indicating no available seats

Both hands chest high, palm open outward, closed fist.

Usher's request for relief

Right hand fact high with index finger touching the temple.

About the Author

Clyde has served as a church usher since early childhood. He served in many capacities, including president, vice president, chairman, and parliamentarian. He had the privilege of organizing many church usher boards. Clyde has served as president of church usher boards for over thirty years.